The Beauty of It

Poems by
Anne Britting Oleson

Anne Britting Oleson

Copyright © 2015 Anne Britting Oleson

ISBN: 0692400087

ISBN-13: 978-0692400081

For Becky, Brenda, Jan & Kasey:
These things are Simply Not Done.

Anne Britting Oleson

CONTENTS

The Beauty of It

ACKNOWLEDGMENTS

"Sculpture" and "The Beauty of It" first appeared in *Animus*.
"Splitting" first appeared in *Boiling River Review*.
"Sleeping with the Red Sox" first appeared in *The Tipton Poetry Journal*.
"Take Me to the River" first appeared in *Willard & Maple*.
"Almost" first appeared in *Red Owl Magazine*.
"First Marriage" first appeared in *The Naugatuck River Review*.
"Divorce" first appeared in *Anthology*.
"Inside, a Thought" first appeared in *Long Story Short*.
"Proposition" first appeared in *Main Street Rag*.

The first edition of *The Beauty of It* was published by Sheltering Pines Press, as the runner-up in their 2010 chapbook contest.

First Marriage

So much grit, caught in the struggling
wind, and you are too weak, too
tired to do this monstrous basket
of wet clothes on your hip any good
at all, should you ever make it
home to the sagging line.

Heavy laundry, but not as heavy as
you are, carrying this nine-month load
low in your pelvis, pain riding the small
of your back that sags, you think,
like the swayed back of the nag
your husband tells you you are.

Before stumbling forward again,
uncertain, your spatulate feet hold
the pavement. At the corner,
the police car. Your brother-in-law
at the wheel, and you flush
with embarrassment to be
so huge, to be washing laundry in public,
to turn down his offer of a lift,
his eyes pitying, the way
they are these days at the sight of you,
with your tight smile and tighter lie:
oh, he's coming, he'll be along.

Splitting

I never used to know anything much
about anything at all, watching
as you chose each piece of wood,
turning it about on the chopping block
with the eye of experience,
until, satisfied, you lifted the maul
above your head and swung
earthward with your entire body.
The halves leapt apart
like magnets of the wrong poles,
and I gathered them for you,
stacking them, as you directed,
ends to the aging sun.

Now I know more, having gained
experience of all kinds
at your square-fingered hands:
I select my wood, looking
for heart shake, the cracks
which radiate from the core.
My own palms blistered, I've learned
how one deliberate blow
can split something
which, until that point,
had been a single, inseparable whole.
I've learned to stack my own fuel
against the coming of a long winter.

Divorce

The night before we were put asunder
you held your head in your hands,
gulping sobs which didn't move me.
At the sink, under the fluorescent ring
I held my back straight to you.

I did not doubt
the sincerity of your anguish.
You truly believed I hurt you
and would stop, if only you cried out;
exactly as I had believed,
each time you swung your fist,
that my tears
would bring you realization.

I studied my hands
through dishwater—scars, a ring,
each considered line—then swirled
a cloth across plates, into cups,
along the blade of a knife.

Inside, a Thought

Salt on ice the length
of the path, dissolving:
tears, then disappointment.
Just rub it into the wound.

The March sun, which ought
to warm, blinds with brightness.
Never mind. Irony is never
lost, except on others.

Was it ever anything other
than winter? Lean into the wind.
Let numbness twist
its ringless fingers.

Burning Over

In this, the spring after you leave, I gather
into a pile all the detritus
of the long cold winter—indeed
of many a past season—
fallen tree limbs, fence rails, rotted floorboards:
everything whose usefulness has passed, everything
I used to think I needed
but which no longer has a place here.
Determined, I set fire to it all.

The blaze might be a funeral pyre,
flames so hungry, so final, devouring the dead
wood I feed it. Or perhaps a suttee,
though I resist any urge on this May evening
alive with apple blossoms and jonquils
to hurl myself onto it:
you would never have suggested
such a drastic measure, I'm sure.

Did you ever burn over, in any of those springs
before me? I've seen you rake anything
that could ignite, and water, and carefully damp
the tip of a cigarette with the hose
before dropping it into your pocket
for later disposal: no.
This fire would have frightened you,
and today, as it devours every offering,
this fire is not for you anyway.

Dead Letter

Envelope unsealed, the paper cuts my finger,
blood whorling the pattern
of the print before staining the page.

The words, too, lie there, stark, scarlet,
and my eyes pick through them like vultures
or grieving relatives searching in vain for kin

among the casualties. A name, even now
calling up the apparition of a once vital,
breathing feeling, hovers over all, a shadow,

a shade. And yet, as I search
through words pleading to be put out
of their misery—*dear* and *caress*

and *heart*—over all I hear that specter,
that name calling mine, over and over,
a piteous wailing, urging me to look back

just once, to return for something
which ought to have been
consigned to the pyre long ago.

Leicester Square

At the corner a woman in a slicker,
shimmering under halogen,
accepts a light from her companion,
who then fires up his own cigarette
and tosses the match to drown in the gutter.
She leans against the lamppost, back arched,
face lifted as she blows the smoke
into the gathering fog.
Her entire posture is an invitation.

Tonight the taxicabs honk
in amiable conversation
far off down in Piccadilly, until
the tires hush themselves
in tired puddles left from the day's rain.
And what of him? His face in shadow,
his hair spiderwebbed by mist,
each strand glittering under the streetlight:
she searches him with her heavy-lidded eyes,
weighing the way he rocks from side
to side on the balls of his feet,
measuring the breadth of his shoulders,
the narrowness of his hips. Their words,
smoky and damp, are only words:
the true conversation flows beneath, a river
of inflection, gesture, as she shifts her gaze upwards,
as he takes a step toward her and away again.

Abruptly she pushes off, and flicks away
the half-done cigarette, heading up
the pavement with arms and hips swinging.
He falls into step beside her, keeping

a careful distance: a dog offered a bone
but knowing a kick might soon follow.

In the Metro

This late in the Paris night the car
stinks of vomit and stale beer.
All seats full, people jockey for that
grudging inch, hanging onto poles,
swinging into each other as the train rounds
one underground corner, then another.
The woman in black across from me
wipes an exhausted hand over her forehead,
lifts her dark hair from her neck.

When I accidentally meet her eyes,
the woman looks away, out the window
into the black void of the tunnel.
Her right hand plays with the gold band,
loose on her wedding finger. Next
to her, a man reads a newspaper,
rustling impatiently as he turns
the page. The woman's eyes do not flicker.

I will her to look up again,
so I can smile, commiserate.
My ring finger is bare.
At the cabaret I sat between
two strangers, toasted them with
champagne as the bare-breasted chorus
danced between French comic routines.
Now, on the Metro, returning to
the narrow hotel room

in the 19th arrondissement, too many
bubbles not yet burst inside,
I want to encourage this woman,
tell her to slough off that expression
so grief-stricken something must have died,
and to slip her hand beneath the news
and caress his leg: come on—
we're in Paris, the City of Love!

The train lurches to a halt at L'Opera
and, so many dominoes, we all tumble
against each other. When our little world
is righted, the stranger with whom
I share the pole has slid his dark hand
down until our fingers touch.
Grinning, he lowers one long-lashed lid.
I know I should glare, snatch my hand away,
but—a glance at the woman in black,
her head leaning against the glass,
her eyes now glittering wetly—I don't.

for Abby Arena

Sculpture

A paperweight in the museum store:
Rodin meant his meaning larger, but
she prefers things she can grasp
with her hands. She traces
fingers along this softness of marble,
measuring a seam between the two figures—
not a seam—a shadow.
Man, woman. Even that is false,
for the two are of one stone.

The fit. Breast to chest, mouth to
bow of lip, hipbone to hipbone,
bend of knee to sweep of thigh.
Hands: between shoulder blades,
in the dip and rise of low back,
along the curve of jaw.

The marble heat of the embrace startles her
through cool stone--she lets it go.
After years, she still feels those hollows
where that one lover locked into her.

Sleeping with the Red Sox

She kept the television on all day,
all night, the first year she lived
alone, without husband
or father. It glowed in its own
room, where she rarely visited.
She never really listened to it talk
to itself, repeating the news
of its day. She only needed
to know it was there, carrying on,
another voice in her otherwise
empty house.

That was then. She's learned to love
the darkness, or at least not
to mind the setting of sun, and can
do without the flickering screen. She's
learned to navigate by touch. Still,
the voices she can't do without:
crawling into this wide bed, she listens
to the team and lulls herself to sleep
with the comfort of the roaring crowd.

Little Domesticities

In the aisle with the flour, sugar,
spices, brownie mixes, he stands,
basket in hand, looking
at crackers, and she catches
her breath at nearly getting
something she really wants.

She can't look into his face.
Her expression would be too plain.
Instead she takes inventory
of his afternoon shopping:
carrots, three cans of soup, two
bottles of red wine.

The distance, then, between
them could not be more
obvious. These little domesticities:
he'll pay, have his necessities
bagged, take them home to life and wife—
far removed from any imaginings
she has a right to have.

13

Proposition

A year since I've seen you, and
two men I know make
offers in the same day. One wheedles:
nobody needs to know. No,
I answer, everyone always finds out.

The other suggests sex
will liven up the friendship.
Or kill it, I can't help reply.

They are both too short. And
married. But this emptiness
warns it wouldn't take much
to change my mind, to tip the
scales in either's direction,

and I'd be back, as I've
been too often, tumbling in
the grass, on a back seat,
somewhere, anywhere, wanting
desperately for it to be you.

Caliban's Lament

I hated him from the first moment:
the corona of his hair searing
my eyes, his features as sharp
as any carved by an artist.
How Prospero's daughter looked upon him,
lips parted, hand light on his arm.
The fire churned in my belly
as I lurked beyond the circle
of their glow, listening to the murmur
of their voices like water over stones.

Monster, she had called me, that day
as my words of love fell between us,
heavy and misshapen, containing
far more than I could make her hear.
Monster, with face as flat
and wounded as a child of Sycorax
could be, wild mat of hair,
hunched back, fisted hands twisting
any attempts at a caress. How could she love
such a thing? And yet—always there,
the hope that she would see
beyond this, into a soul
warm as summer rain, and would place
her delicate fingers in my hand.
Yet the more I pleaded, the further away
she drew, her face creased
and shadowed in revulsion.

Now she smiles upon this beautiful stranger
while my insides twist into knots
I'll never untangle. He professes devotion
in words clear enough even for my ears:
my heart in his mouth.

Poem

He reads aloud a poem
translated from another language
about a man emptying his pockets
onto a table
until it becomes full
until it becomes the universe

and as he reads, morning
cedes to winter afternoon
with sun angling
through French doors
slicing red across wallpaper
until it just grazes the tips
of his fingers on the book
and I know what it is
to want all the things I can't name
listening to his low voice,
holding my breath.

Take Me to the River

Just after sunset. The Mohawk Trail narrows
to pot-holed opposing lanes, twisting
upwards into the Berkshires, lonely miles linked
by gleams of light through uncurtained windows,
the glittering beads on an undulating chain.

Driving blues from the radio, sounds
more tender after nightfall
than under the glare of noon. I reach
for your hand, skin cool, smooth, bones
delicate as a swallow's. Exhausted
in the worry of the unknown,
you sleep away the darkening miles,
your face a pale moon in the flash
of headlights from a pickup
turning into a lonesome bar.

A sigh escapes, the sound
like the murmur of the Connecticut running
alongside lilacs in the dark.

The Beauty of It

Surprising beauty in unlikely places.
This afternoon, white smile, dark skin:
the hard-hatted man weaving his hands
through the elevator wiring in the grime
of South Station, plucking the strands
as though at the strings of a harp, or
at my own heartstrings, for that matter,
as he offers to lug my suitcase down
two flights of stairs to the subway platform.
I love this man. He must know it. As much,
perhaps, as I love the waiter twenty years
my junior, his black hair tumbling
over his black eyes as he pours Beaujolais
under the awning on Montmartre,
both of us looking forward to the intimate
moment when we link fingers and press
that secret coinage from palm to palm, skin
warm, tip cool. In some place
of longing beneath my walking from work
to the bus stop, from the bus stop to home,
I know: they are out there, jewels
littering the path, men to make my blood
pound, my skin tingle. Like the sweet fruit
inside the prickly outer shell, they demand
the work of looking. Just as the poet,
after the dissolution of the master class,
when we slipped into the whiteness of a light

snow, leaned in the car window to kiss
my cheek as a snowflake might in its drifting.

Not Quite

Crescent moon floats overhead.
They lie together and apart under
the star-spattered blanket of sky.
He smokes. She watches the filminess
ease its way upward, thinning
into nothingness.

If she turns her head, she might press
her lips to the pale skin of his inner arm
where the elbow crooks to cradle
his head. An invitation.
But she won't, and knows it, smiling
to herself as he breathes the coal
end of the cigarette red. She will not
kiss him, or touch him, or shed her clothes.
It is not what she wants—

the complications, the inevitable
recriminations, the destruction
of this easy companionability
that even now requires no words.
No. The morning to follow
will bring no regrets. The breeze
lifts the hair from her brow, soft
as a touch, and she amuses herself
with the thought while he
smokes on under the stars.

ABOUT THE AUTHOR

Anne Britting Oleson is a Pushcart-Prize-nominated poet and novelist who lives and writes in the mountains of Central Maine. Her other books include *The Church of St. Materiana* (poetry), *Planes and Trains and Automobiles* (poetry), and *The Book of the Mandolin Player* (novel).

www.ingramcontent.com/pod-product-compliance
Lightning Source LLC
Chambersburg PA
CBHW060605030426
42337CB00019B/3611